CAN WE TALK?

AND OTHER POEMS

Book design by Leif Södergren

Cover drawing by Donovan O'Malley

AUTHOR'S NOTE
I want to express my deepest appreciation to Donovan O'Malley, artist,
novelist, and playwright, for his generous permission to use his artwork to
illustrate several of the poems in this collection. My further appreciation
and gratitude goes to Leif Sodergren, my editor, designer, and producer
of this and of my previous collection, "The Buzzards' Roost."
These are collaborations, professional and personal, that I treasure.

ISBN
978-91-982015-9-8

contact:
lemongulch@yahoo.com

LEMONGULCHBOOKS
www.lemongulchbooks.com

CAN WE TALK?

AND OTHER POEMS

BEASLEY LEFFEW

CONTENTS

STEADFAST
In memory
Willa Dean Gore Leffew

He was her life's love, trouble as he was.
There was a wildness in his heart,
Some longing that he chased
Through all their long years together,

She didn't know what thing he sought,
What restlessness called him from her
And made him disappear, time and again.
She'd tolerate his absence for a while

Then, steadfast, would go out to find him.
And when his final absence came
She sat down one day, closed her eyes,
Went out to find him one last time.

SOMETIMES I DREAM I AM AIR

Sometimes I dream I am air
air that is breathed by a plunging horse
air that becomes blood of the beast
coursing through the great heart
and all its tributaries air expelled
from its heaving lungs to become
again air that feeds a fire huge
forest fire precursor of greening life
from later rain that puts out
the fire nourishing new growth
out of the earth to become a leaf
that gives off air that's breathed
by a plunging horse and so it goes
through the eons so what I am now
this earthbound puny dreamer
is just a phase I'm going through
a process of infinite permutations
where all comes 'round
and nothing is lost

HARBINGER

Deep in Winter, a suddenly mild day;
Trees form a tracery of black bone-bare limbs
Against a banging blue sky. The sun warms
The campus walk I take toward the quad,
Where girls emerge like Spring flowers,
Some in shorts, their legs crocus-white,
Or brown as beach sand. Barefoot boys
Sail a frisbee, robin's breast red, through
The crystalline air.

I, three-quarters century of age,
Feeling the lingering chill,
Wrapped in cap and coat, scarf and gloves,
Approach this scene, a winter wind on a warmish day,
Am by youth observed, but not perceived -
Until one day, years hence, they awake
With a heaviness in the limbs, a new chill in the bone,
An old ache in the heart, and remember -
How strange to recall -

On that sweet day in the quad, so full of sun and youth,
An old man wrapped in winter coming toward them.

I BOUGHT A BOOK

I bought a book, an empty journal
In which to record my thoughts
But the clear pages with the lovely
Blue lines and waiting spaces between
Were so beautiful I had nothing to say
Beyond what wasn't there

So I bought a book full of others' thoughts,
Thoughts so beautiful and profound
That I was inspired to think again and the wish
To write my own thoughts came upon me
So I bought another book, an empty journal
With beautiful blue lines and silent spaces

And found in that limitless emptiness
Nothing more to say.

THE HERALD

I often see them, these two, walking on the trail:
The old man and his dog, she always going before
And always carrying in her mouth a long black stick.

It has meaning for her, this leading, this carrying;
It is her work, preceding her human in the unvarying ritual
Of their walk; the stick she carries is a staff of office,

A necessary part of her work as herald
More eloquent than words, her look at me says
"Make way! Make way! The King! The King!"

IN THE HERB GARDEN

Common Sage, they call me.
I try not to be offended, remembering
How humans have this odd need
To name things. But common!
How ordinary are they who call me so?

I was not thought common by the Romans,
Who looked to me for cures of everything
From ague to toothache. Nor by the Greeks,
Who had faith in my powers to bestow longevity.
Now, however, I am deemed useful only in the kitchen.

Nevertheless, I endure, here in my corner of the garden.
The winters are merciless. Parsley, my poor neighbor,
Makes attempt to live, but rarely survives. Thyme,
Another neighbor, usually pulls through, but emerges
Maimed in Spring.

The early frost took sweet Basil, altering his fragrant beauty
Into darkened wilt. Such inevitable change saddens me.
Friends Oregano and Chive prudently disappear
Into root underground, snug beneath the snow and ice,
And emerge refreshed, come Spring. I am cheered by their
return.

The years, the wintry trials and losses, pass. I endure.
For herbs and humans, a kind of common heroism.

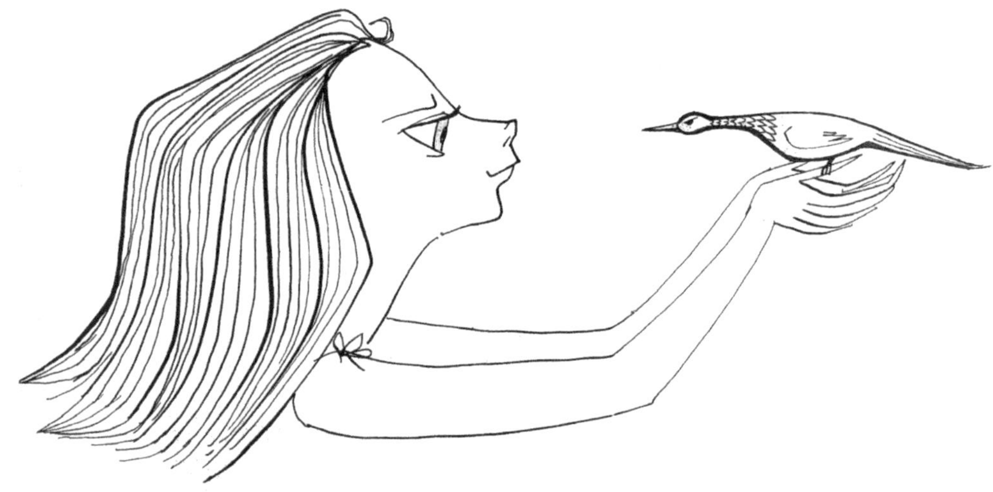

MOCKINGBIRD

1.
Yes, there are predators that keep me on guard,
Food to find, nests to build, chicks to hatch and feed.
Life has its cares and cautions - But ah!

The exuberance! To fling oneself out
Into the insubstantial air, to be lifted in flight,
To fill that air with joyous song from a repertoire
That all the world, including you, humans, envy.

I am the diva. My complicated arias have stopped
Farmers in their fields to hear my songs,
Halted cats in their murderous prowl.
Such joy! To fly, to sing, to know only Now!

2.
Bird, fly in to my heart
Sing it full of joyous song
Teach this poor human
To know only Now

GRAVITY
For Sir Isaac Newton (1642-1727)

Newton sat under an apple tree
And there discovered gravity
When an apple fell upon his head
"Eureka! Fnet=m.a," he said.

Just imagine his elation
At working out this equation-
And proving that he wasn't eccentric
In thinking our cosmos heliocentric!

Gravity's the thing, he said,
That lets us lie upon our bed
Instead of floating up above it
It's universal - you gotta love it!

It keeps us on the ground while joggin'
And keeps our hat upon our noggin;
And how would our peas stay on our plate
If they could not gravitate?

Or how, pray tell, could we get a drink
Of water, not an easy thing, I think,
Instead of the way it usually flows
It's apt to pour right up your nose.

There'd be no end to daily trials:
We'd hit a baseball forty miles;
We couldn't sit without a tether
We'd be airborne in windy weather.

You couldn't even ride a horse
Without the gravitational force;
The beast would bounce you over the moon
And you'd land somewhere in Saskatoon.

But there'd be one good thing, I guess:
We all would weigh a whole lot less,
But all in all I'd say it's great
That here on earth we gravitate.

Newton's discovery was profound
And influenced the whole world 'round;
But he brought us something else as big:
A delicious cookie made of fig.

THE PRAIRIE SEA - SUMMER

No mountains here, nor ocean's rocky shore,
Nor roaring chasm, nor gorge's river'd floor;
A glacier raked this earth to sculpted plains.

Yet something of the ancient sea remains
In dip and fall of land, and swell and lift;
In scattered sand and stone and pebbled drift

Of ancient sea floor carved into moraine.
The long slow roll of sunlit green terrain,
The billowed bulge of surging greening grain

Subsides in frothing surf of Queen Anne's lace
Along a shore of fenceline. In this place
The land becomes the ancient sea again.

AUBADE

The morning sun has burst into my room,
Unwelcome messenger that's come to call
Me from my blissful dreams, haul me away
From out my snuggy bed into a day
That's far too real for me, for after all,
My artist's soul does not awake 'til noon.

So let me dream of waves that lap a beach,
Where tropic birds do grace the morn with song-
There is no birdsong here, only a roar
That's coming from a lawnmower next door.
My unforgiving clock says move along;
Ah well - once more, dear friends, unto the breach.

But thinking of the day that lies ahead,
I feel it's best if I just stay in bed.

BIRDLAND

First, the cardinals at daybreak,
They that tolerate everyone except each other;
Later on, en famille, the cheery sparrows,
Gregarious and sociable to dine, followed by
A communal bath:"Everybody in the pool!"
And then fly off together for more fun.
The jays, loud and aggressive,
Chase all others away to take command
Of the feeder; pugilistic pose. Once gone
Come the doves, flying in on squeaking wings
That sound rusty, in need of oiling; they call
Something that sounds like great alarm:
"Omigod! The ground's coming up so fast!"
Joining them briefly, the chickadee
Prefers take-out to eating in; she picks a seed
And flies off to dine alone, away from the proles
At the feeder. And one early evening, there was
A small owl that settled near where I sat,
And her gaze of calm indifference, or disdain,
Seemed to say,"Look at you. You can't even fly."
As if flight were not the most magical thing
One could imagine. A little later, the last to return,
The cardinals came to close the day and call a
Good night, good night sweet, sweet day.
We live for the morrow.

OLD SCHOOL

I know that these days anything goes
In daily discourse and in poetry and prose;
But deep within my soul I balk
When I hear the awful way you talk.

So listen up, people, I have some complaints:
I've had it with listening to your "ain'ts"
When "aren't'" or "isn't" are no harder to say;
And while we're at it, ditch "no way."

Furthermore, such joy if you'd simply say,
"Ultimately," instead of "at the end of the day."
And such a relief if we never heard
"Like" between every other word.

(Will someone please tell me how
To interpret the phrase, "I go, like, wow!")
And anyone who's over the age of nine
Who utters "Awesome!" should pay a fine.

There's more: I would feel truly blessed
If you figured out how to use "few" and "less":
The fewer (plural) such gaffes I see,
The less (singular) irritated I will be.

And while we're at it, here's a good place
To consider the objective case:
As objects, "him" and "me" won't do
'Til a verb or preposition precedes the two.

Moreover, I can't suppress a frown
When I hear you use the wrong pronoun.
"Him and me won the football pool"
Confirms you slept your way through school

You need work on the subjunctive mood:
I really wish you understood
That "If I were you" is the hypothetical;
"If I was you" is just pathetical.

Sorry, no, I'm not quite done;
You have to stop saying "Have a good one."
One what? Good life? Good root canal?
It's a wish as empty as it is banal.

Now, here I really have to beg:
Eschew the double neg
ative, and if you would,
Stop splitting infinitives like kindling wood,

And ending sentences with prepositions.
People, heed this admonition:
Stamp out these horrors with an emphatic foot;
There are some things
               up with which
                   I will not
                       put.

AUBADE
(AT BREAKFAST)

Morning pours sunlight upon the table
Like golden pancake syrup, accidentally spilled.
The silver kettle is filled, waiting for me
To make the tea. I take up the widowed yellow cup,
Its saucer recently deceased (victim of pitiless gravity),
And from the tea tin place within the morning oolong.
The kettle's shrill song, a whistle powered by steam,
(It has locomotive dreams) calls to me:
"Water's ready! Make the tea!" I hasten to obey
This summons; otherwise, the day, so far,
Is a pandemonium of steam and noise. From the drawer,
I take up my favorite knife, my santoku, and poise
To cleave an orange or two; and then, into the toaster's maw,
Two slices of bread, to be spread with butter, when browned.
Presently, there erupts a Jack-In-The Box hilarity
Of breakfast acrobatics: toast is tossed into the air
From out the sprung machine, as if shot from a cannon:
Circus dramatics! Close at hand stand the sturdy shakers,
And that rash eloping couple, the dish and the spoon,
Back from their honeymoon, are set
Beside a virgin serviette, which, unsullied, yet trembles
For the wet kiss of buttery lips. It is my wish
This day, that whatever kitchen gods it may please
Grant that I be useful as all of these.

AT THE MARKET

As I place my purchases on the counter
The clerk asks pleasantly, "Did you
Find what you were looking for?"
"I did, thanks," I reply.

Rote question, perfunctory reply,
Meaningless exchange. And yet…
Making my way across the parking lot,
Burdened by what I've bought,

The question takes on an importance,
A poignance, redolent of last things
A question one might well ask
As a final summing-up:

Did you find what you were looking for?

I may have seen, but not perceived it
I may have touched, but not felt it
I may have grasped, but not held it
Did you find what you were looking for?

I don't know

THE SKEPTIC CONTEMPLATES FAITH

I
Hebrews 11:1

Kneeling in a sharp November wind,
My head bowed in concentration,
It may well be supposed, seen from afar,
That I am at prayer. I smile at the irony,
As I do not pray. Still, it is perhaps
A kind of prayer with which I genuflect
To plant each bulb, an act of faith
That I will be graced to see its secrets
 Bloom into an unseen Spring.

II
Matthew 17:20

It doesn't look like much, this tiny seed I hold for planting.
Brown, desiccated, an unlikely-looking prospect for greatness.
And yet this tiny dot, scarcely more than a shadow, holds a great
Amazement: that so small a speck holds so large a thing as life.

It holds as well, the Bible tells us, Faith. And, while Matthew's mustard seed
Held faith in the kingdom of Heaven, I think this seed holds with Nature,
Giving us, as here, the vision to see greatness in small things.
So it's a collaboration we have: I plant this seed with faith in its potential,

And it gives me something important to contemplate: that some sense
May be made of this random ride on a spinning roulette-wheel world
If one has faith such as this: faith that Nature's laws are ineffable
And immutable and always bend toward what should be;

Faith that a belief in things unseen may be found in a cathedral,
Or in something as improbable - impossible, even, as this tiny seed.

LOVE SONG
For J.

Let us go then, let's be matey
Now that I'm approaching eighty
I need a friend with me to wend
Through half-deserted streets that end
In a sawdust restaurant somewhere,
Me with a bald spot usurping my hair.
There, among villains and strumpets,
We shall take our tea and crumpets.
Oh do not ask what it may be-
Right now I really need to pee.

In the room the woman comes and goes
Smoking a pack of Marlboros.

Shall I squeeze the universe into a ball?
Age has weakened my grip, after all,
But still I grasp at those compelling

Questions that are overwhelming:
Shall I eat a stew of prune?
Shall I go howling at the moon?
What about my balding pate?
What is left to celebrate?

I dither, I dither, I know not whither
My mind is going; I know it's slowing.

But indeed there may be time, I note
While the Eternal Footman holds my coat,
Time for me and time for you,
Time to eat a pruney stew
To keep most regular our bowels.
Time to rake the moon with howls.

In the room the woman comes and goes
Blowing smoke rings out her nose.

And indeed there may be time
To turn and descend the stair
By means of this mechanical chair;
I'll hide my own Easter eggs
Then try to find them, if my legs
Support me through such adventure
And, if I can find my denture,

I'll dare to eat a green banana
I'll rent a beachside cabana
I'll bid the mermaids come ashore
And sing to me at last, before
I say, ere I close my eyes,
Mr. Eliot, I do apologize.

CAN WE TALK?

You'd like to hear from me? How sweet!
I'd like to hear from you.
You know, we could always tweet,
On twitter - that's what I do.

Call you on the telephone?
How quaint, and so old school.
Send an email to your home?
LOL! Uncool.

Meet someplace for a cup of joe,
And have a face to face?
I face to face on Facebook, so
I'll friend you from my place.

Send you a letter in the mail?
That just won't do at all.
U knw vry well that I cn't spell
I'll text you from the mall.

Could we shake hands and just be friends?
I think that would be great,
But my smartphone's grown into my hand.
They'd have to amputate.

A Haiku Year

<u>New Year's Day</u>

Church bell ringing out
Signals a beginning and
Stirs old memories

<u>Kyoto, April</u>
    1963
Cherry blossoms float
On the rippled gravel waves
At Ryoan-ji

<u>Sommer Nachtmusik</u>

Crickets fiddle, frogs
Sing arias to the moon.
Summer night music!

<u>Nightwind</u>

Autumn wind at night.
My thoughts scatter like dry leaves
Blown through empty streets

GOLD

Sitting on a Napa Valley terrace,
Sipping a glass of straw-colored Chardonnay,
I watch the vineyards turn blue in fading light
Slanting across the gently undulating hills.

The yellow mustard blooms among the vines
Bring to mind the gold of Southern fields
In autumn when the lowering sun
Turned the fields I wandered into a golden flood

Of yellowed leaves. And at their harvest,
The crops of hay and straw were bound
Into gigantic rolls, like balls on a leveled lawn,
Awaiting giants to come and play croquet.

A sip, not of wine, but of childhood memory
When giants came out to play.

VINTAGE

This glass holds a wine that tastes like the scent
of cypress trees on the beach at Carmel,
the bouquet a soft ocean fog tinged with smoke
from the fire we sat by at ocean's edge
and watched how the rising sparks became
stars strewn across the midnight sky.
This glass holds that evening
by the purpled sea, the vintage
aged in memory, cellared in the heart.

MAKE THE WIND MY HOME

Though I have loved this earth, I have no wish
To be mewed up inside her dark embrace;
Pass me through the purifying fire
Thus transformed into a rarer state,

Put me on the wind, that I might race
To fill a sail or wave a summer leaf,
Draw bright music from tinkling chimes
I set astir in headlong flight.

Make the wind my home, offer me up
To that from which I came,
Let a sunlit pine whisper my name.

EDWARD HOPPER'S "MORNING SUN"

The room holds a vast silence,
A melancholy quality of light
That sets a mood resigned
As the figure on the bed, who stares
Onto a row of windows that stare back
Sightless windows offering blankness
Nothing else.

Voyeur! You've felt this silence,
This emptiness, have sat on your bed
Faced the indifferent day
And wondered if it mattered
If you arose or not.

The artist knew all this.
Look on her. And see yourself.

FAMILY ALBUM
JOINED IN HAIKU

James Elisha Leffew
"Pap"
I sired this sprawl, this
chaos of family, my
life's richest harvest.

Susie Elizabeth Adams Leffew
"Mam"
Harvest required sons.
I bore his brood. All the while,
poems sang in me.

Shelvin
Me? Never married.
Why buy the cow when you can
have the milk for free?

Herschel
Free? I gave nothing
free; as little profit there
As in a bird's song.

Nell
Songs of love I sang,
and love was my undoing.
He killed me. Love's strange.

Louis
Strange how I, in the
prime of my life, one night heard
an owl call my name.

Elva
"Name one thing-bet you
can't-I can't do well." Can you
stop talking? "Name two."

Christine
Two husbands, and both
loved to dance. I miss them so
I can't stop dancing.

Carrie
Dancing! At her age!
And she twice widowed! I've no
time for such nonsense.

Russel
Nonsense, tall tales and
Thin baloney - that's all I
Get at Blackjack Store.

Tom
Stores of questions: folks
Ask"I wonder what happened
to him?" So do I.

Eddy
I placed my picture
on Mam's mantle. But I know
Floyd's her brown-eyed boy.

Shelly
Boy, how we would fight,
as brothers will do. But when
Floyd died, my heart broke.

Floyd
Broke, while my brothers
prospered. All I had was love.
I died a rich man.

George
Man, life's a party!
Sick, sober, sorry; but look
at the fun I've had!

SEEKING INSPIRATION

No epiphanies today.
The door to perception is firmly closed.
A small placard hangs on its handle:

"Back at: "
and underneath,

A little clock face
    with
      only
      one
      hand

RIDDLES

1.

My face shows neither pain nor pleasure.
My hands hold, mete out and measure
A priceless treasure

2.

As we glide gracefully into view,
No one can tell between us two
Which is me, and which is you.

3.

My military rank you can easily tell.
At listening, I'm equipped to excel.
I make a fine chicken dinner as well!

4.

Although I've only one foot, I'm admired
For my rhythmic gait, and when inspired
I can go many meters and never get tired.

1. Clock; 2. Dance; 3. Corn; 4. Iamb

A WINTER'S TALE

I don't like that young man
daughter's going with, He said.
Whyever not? He seems like
a perfectly nice boy, She said.

Not so nice, He said. I saw where
 he pee'd his name in the snow.
Oh what of that, She said.
That's just something boys do.

Yes, but it was daughter's handwriting,
He said.
OH. She said.

THE NEWS AT 80

Well, he was old, they will say,
Reading of him in the morning obits,
It was time for him to move along.

Others make the news this day,
Felled by accident or fits
Of bodily infirmity, or by chance,

Or who, perhaps in spirited dance
Suddenly left this life behind. It sits
Heavy on the heart, these songs unsung;

Our bodies age, but we all die young.

NABOKOV IN MIDNIGHT'S HOUSE

In midnight's house reproach hangs batlike
from the rafters spidery remorse skitters across
empty floors regret coils yellow-eyed in a cobweb
corner and should-have-done's scritch and scratch
inside the walls while in the library Mr. Nabokov
in a silk smoking-jacket seated reads:

    The cradle rocks above an abyss

Darkness seeps into the room
three crows fly through the uncurtained window
their calls are echoes in a stone chamber
where each beat of my pounding heart says
tictoc
      tic toc
           tic

HALCYON DAYS
for Donovan O'Malley

We're in the same boat, my dear old friend,
Drifting on a stream of days, we take
More and more from less and less; we keep
A sailor's watch for what may lie ahead-
A raging waterfall, or else a shore
With dappled shade. In either case, it seems
We're in for more adventure yet, and so

Hoist up the Jolly Roger! And break out
The sparkling wine! Now that the sun's below
The yard, we'll drink the health of absent friends
And to those halcyon days of sun and youth
That shine across the years to bring us joy.
And though we drift in late season, all's well:
The halcyon builds her nest in winter days.

IN THE GARDEN

The things I planted grow in orderly fashion,
Straight and tall in disciplined rows. I bend to pull
The encroaching weeds, but a memory stays my hand:
"Y'all kids are growing like weeds," my father said;
Which is to say, we grew not only fast, but wild,
Seeking root wherever the wind might blow us.

No regimented rows of pampered plants were we:
Untended by loving but laissez-faire parents
We grew weed-like as Nature would have it,
Following whatever sun seemed to shine for us,
Often landing in places where we didn't belong
Until finally finding a welcoming nest of nettles
With thick skins and hearts soft as thistledown
And calling it home.

ECLIPSE

Selene, goddess of the moon,
Got in her brother Helios' way;
She darkened his bright shining noon
And spread her nighttime o'er his day.

Their sister Eos primly sat
And stayed her dawn until these two
Were finished with their sibling spat
And, since they were not yet through,

The Bears, who sensed no coming dawn,
Resumed their lope across dark space;
Orion woke with a mighty yawn,
Took up his sword, resumed his chase.

Thus while the gods their drama played,
Earth's creatures warred in ancient shade.

EARLY ONE MORNING

Early one morning I rose from my bed,
Leaving my sleeping body behind, emptied of me.
I saw myself an insubstantial form
Released from living physicality
Into another plane, transformed,
Ethereal as the air I no longer breathed.

I thought perhaps I'm dying now, and - odd-
I felt no fear or dread; there was instead
An intense curiosity, a wish to know
What awaited in my transformed state.

Oh keep religion's grasping hands away:
There are no gods behind this sense of mine
That I stood at a frontier's edge and glimpsed
Amid the haze, a Beyond with no horizon.

THE CRONE
For Pearlie Bilbrey

Aunt Pearlie Bilbrey was an ancient crone
Always in black, hunched, with a hopping gait,
Crow's feet lining her hawk-billed face
With piercing black eyes, amused, wise.

My dad, giving her a ride one day, said
"Pearlie, you look like a ole black crow
Hopping out across the yard."

She laughed her cackling, cawing laugh,
Got into his car, and with a rustle
Like that of folding wings,
Settled herself into her nest of a seat.

Menaced by deepnight doubts, I conjure
Pearlie and her magic to hurry the dawn.
Wise old crone or crow,
Impart some wisdom to my dreams.

AUGURY

In a chair by the garden
I watch late afternoon shadows
Slant across the lawn, while overhead
Vultures from a committee under the hill
Glide in their daily reconnoiter.

Lazily drifting in a lazuli sky,
Light winking on their great underwings,
Flashing semaphore I cannot read,
They ride on thermals that lift them in dreamy
flight,
Rise and fall as on ocean swells they sail
In feathered whispers.

The ancients revered these creatures,
Sacred to Isis, the Dakini,
Embodiment of highest wisdom,
Messengers whose flight bore omens:

Oh you who are bound to Earth,
Do not ask of our augury what is to come;
Do not ask, "Will I?" Ask instead, "Am I?"
Self-knowledge is the beginning of wisdom.

FIRST CROCUS

Tiny white soldiers, the advance flank
Of more colorful comrades to come,
Stand bravely against the February wind.
Gathered in a small bed of green, circled
As if for safety, or comfort, or strength
From the winter wind that blasts them
They shiver, yet how cheerful they seem
In each other's company. In their bright
Array against the darkling afternoon
They dance in the sharp wind, call out
"Be of good cheer, Spring will come again!
We are its eternal promise."

LAO-TZU AT THE HOCKEY GAME

In combination of grace and violence
Large men on skates chase at frantic speed
A small disk skittering over ice
Toward a net guarded by a masked gorgon
Encouraged by a screaming crowd.

In the midst of this chaos sits Lao-Tzu
Slightly bored and smiling quietly, he remarks

The Tao says do not contend, but here
All is contention, a vain effort where
Man has turned water, which benefits
The ten thousand things, into ice for combat.
Best to be like water.

RESURRECTION

It requires unquestioning faith to believe
The myth received; and Reason asks:
On what evidence?

Yet, there do exist intangible realities
In which faith may be placed, and Reason
May accommodate:

That a rose lies humming beneath the Winter snow;
That from out the dead leaf a butterfly will ascend;
That the skeletal trees thrum with unseen life arising.

Hummingbirds will return with Spring;
The sun will rise, as human spirits do
When frailty is overcome.

An addict defeats his demons, and is restored to life;
Old hurts are forgiven, restoring friendship to life;
Beauty lifts up the spirit, transcendent, restoring hope and faith.

And love that lifts the heart in ascending joy.
The wondrous world abounds in resurrection,
Ancient myth translated to blazing life.

RAKING LEAVES ON HALLOWEEN

Nature shows her humor most,
Or is it irony
To trick out summer's fallen ghosts
In vivid livery?

Like putting rouge upon the dead
To make them less a fright,
She paints them up in gold and red
To swirl in whirlwind flight.

And when these wraiths have quit their flight
I pile them for a pyre;
When look! Within the pile a light,
A ray of green leaf fire!

Sly magic trick on Halloween,
This future April's wink of green.

AT THE PASSPORT OFFICE

Contemplating his renewal picture he sees a different traveller,
a stranger ten years along, the wanderings of the past decade
imprinted on his face like a customs agent's stamp, the lines
and wrinkles rivers mapping the foreign country of the past
where he lingered too long, apprehensive about continuing
his journey into another decade which will take him
well into his nineties - is it outrageous optimism or absurd hope
to think that he will journey for another decade while so many other
journeys have been cut short? And what borders will he cross
until he arrives at that frontier where he surrenders
his passport for a permanent visa, becomes a citizen
of a new land, a synchronicity where time and space
are crude concepts of a former dimension; newborn as stardust,
he sails oceans of deepest mystery in a strange and borderless country
where no papers are required.

PHOTOS AND ILLUSTRATIONS

Illustrations:
Donovan O'Malley:
Pages: 1,4,6,8,10,13,14,16,18,20,22,24,30,
35,39,40,42,45,47,50,53,56 and 63.

Christina Cini: p.2

Photos:
Leif Södergren:
Pages: 27, 32, 36, 61

Family archives:
p. 48 and 54

Lady Ottoline Morrell (1934):
p.29